Creative Bible Games

For All Ages

By Judy Dorsett

Illustrated by Ed Koehler

Cincinnati, Ohio

Cover and inside illustrations by Ed Koehler

Scriptures [marked ICB] quoted from the *International Children's Bible, New Century Version,* copyright © 1986, 1988 by Word Publishing, Dallas, Texas 765039. Used by permission.

© 1998 by The Standard Publishing Company
Revised and published in 1998 by The Standard Publishing Company, Cincinnati, Ohio
A division of Standex International Corporation
All rights reserved
Printed in the United States of America

05 04 03 02 01 00 99 98   5 4 3 2 1

ISBN 0-7847-0741-3

Contents

Games Galore	4
Get Acquainted Games	5
Getting to Know You	6
Simple Scripture Board Games	7
Scorecards	8
Around the Church	9
A Big Fish Tale	10
The Great Race	11
The Sower	12
The Lost Son	13
The Builder	14
In the Vine	15
Question Card Games	16
"B" is for Bible	18
One Another	25
Honeycomb	31
Play Ball!	36
Bingo Games	39
Overhead Projector Games	42
Initial Blocks	43
Screen Scrabble	47

Games Galore
Ideas to Help You Use This Book

Games provide a great opportunity to teach, reinforce, and review learning! They also encourage class members' participation, interaction among players and leaders, and delight in the learning environment.

The games in this book include complete instructions, game boards, question cards, scorecards, overhead projector transparency masters, and helpful tips to aid the teacher and involve class members.

Most games include sample question cards as well as blank forms so teachers can create their own versions based on current lessons or materials.

This smorgasbord of games ranges from get-acquainted games to Scripture and parable games; from question-card games to overhead projector games. They can be adapted for early readers through adults, for use in a wide range of settings. You can write simple questions and read the questions to nonreaders.

Use the games for teaching Scripture and Scripture concepts, for reviewing lesson information, for breaking the ice in new classrooms or at workshops, and for building rapport among students and teachers.

Teachers want to reach their students with the message of God's love and care. They want class members to enjoy the learning process and each other. They want to be creative and add variety to current lessons. Games are a tool that can make all these goals possible!

Tips and Resources for Using These Adaptable Games

Game boards—Photocopy onto white or colored paper or card stock. Preserve them with clear plastic adhesive or lamination.

Question cards—Photocopy onto white or colored paper or card stock. Match the color of the game board to the color of the question cards to keep various game parts together. Cut apart and place each card set in an envelope.

Move tokens—Education supply stores sell small colored plastic circles and tokens. Colored buttons or play money coins are usable.

Move indicators—Spinners (borrow from other game sets or purchase from education supply store), dice, or coins. (Decide how many spaces to move for "heads" and how many for "tails.")

Bingo markers—Colored construction paper squares and dried beans are two easy options. Dry snacks (cereal, crackers) can be used for a snack while the game is being played!

Overhead transparencies—Purchase blank transparencies and use the transparency master provided with the game. Specialty stores can prepare these if you do not have access to a photocopy machine that makes transparencies.

Get Acquainted Games

Breaking the ice is important to newly formed groups of people! Most of us feel more accepted and we are more willing to take part in a new group when we become acquainted with others. It may take more than one such activity over several weeks to encourage communication and friendship.

Getting to Know You

Getting to Know You game grid page 6

Getting to Know You invites people to share general, sometimes humorous, information. It can also be used to discover more specific and personal information. Teachers and group leaders tailor these games to fit their classes. Depending on the items chosen and the reading level difficulty, they are adaptable to any age.

Photocopy the master grid (page 6). Type phrases chosen for the game and photocopy this new page so that each class member will have one. Save the photocopy master for reuse.

When choosing items for the game card, include a few obvious things such as hair color as well as things that players must tell about themselves such as birthplace, birth date, and so on. The objective is for people to talk among themselves. You want the interaction to be informative and somewhat personal. Use your imagination! Changing items enables reuse of the game with the same group.

Sample instructions

"Each of you has a game grid and a pencil. Talk with one another to discover people who fit each category. When you find someone with the 'more than 2 pets,' for example, have him write his name in that square. The first person to fill in all the squares wins!"

General information ideas
- more than 2 pets
- hair (color, length)
- eyes (color)
- picture of family in pocket or purse
- tallest, shortest, etc.
- wearing most (color)
- birthday closest to (Christmas, today's date)
- born out of state
- more than 20 coins in pocket or purse
- rides bus #
- biggest or smallest (Bible, purse)

Find out a little about each class member to compile this list. Use phrases that would complete a question: "Who . . . ?"
- works in a (bank, school, etc.)
- plays the (piano, guitar, etc.)
- drives a (color and type of car)
- has (# of) children
- enjoys (hobby)
- traveled to
- used to live in (city, state)
- vacationed in (destination)
- lives at (address)
- was born in
- volunteers at
- loves to (read, ride horses, etc.)

Getting to Know You

Simple Scripture Board Games

Photocopy game boards—one for each group of players. You can photocopy some of the games on colored paper.

Spin a spinner, roll a die, or flip a coin (heads move 2; tails move 3).

Provide a game move token for each player.

Directions for each game are on the game form.

Church Helpers Game

This game reminds players that everyone in the church is important. It helps them identify many opportunities for service.

Before the game begins, teachers should help the group make a list of service activities.

Because this game requires only the ability to count and move a token, nonreaders can enjoy playing it, too.

Scripture Games

These games teach the main points or events of the Scripture as players move around the game board. Players read the phrases aloud when they land on them.

A Big Fish Tale reviews the story of Jonah's rebellion against God (Jonah 1, 2, 3).

The Great Race highlights what Christians ought to remember as they live their lives for God (Hebrews 12).

Parable Games

These games showcase the truths Jesus taught in parables. Players read the phrases aloud as they land on the spaces. Sometimes players are asked to explain the meaning of parable parts or the entire parable.

Around the Church game board
page 9

A Big Fish Tale game board
page 10

The Great Race game board
page 11

The Sower game board
page 12

The Lost Son game board
page 13

The Builder game board
page 14

In the Vine game board
page 15

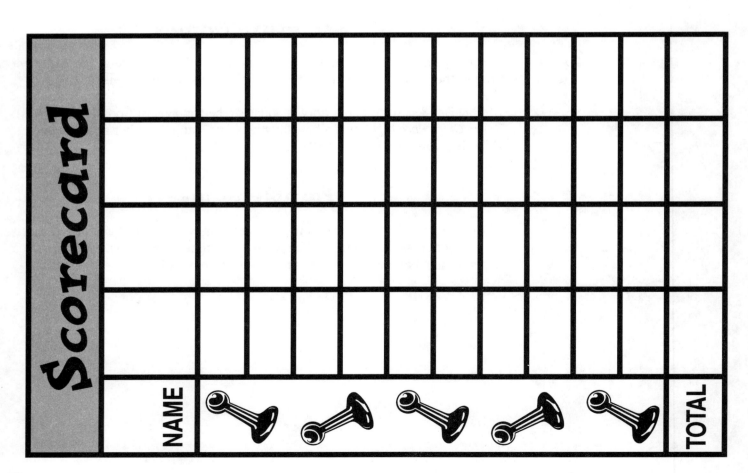

Around the Church...

Let's name some ways to serve God!

Before beginning to play, brainstorm a list of jobs and ministries people do in the church. Spin a spinner, roll a die, or toss a coin (heads, 2; tails, 3). Move the number of spaces indicated. Take turns moving until a player reaches the church. When each player moves, he must call out a job not yet named during the game. The game winner is the first one to reach the church, but we all win when we serve God!

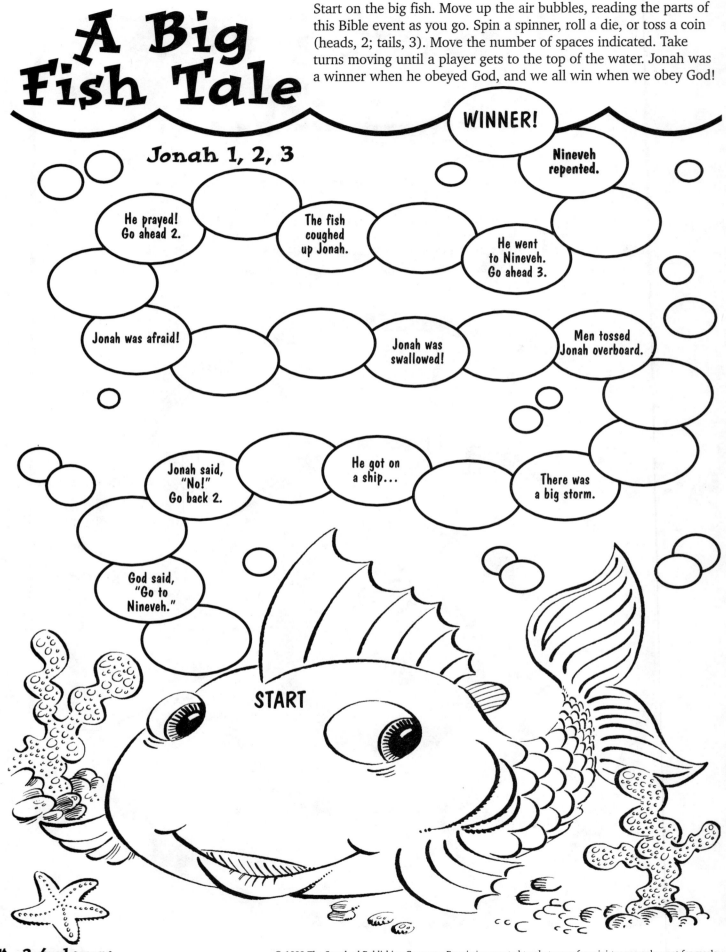

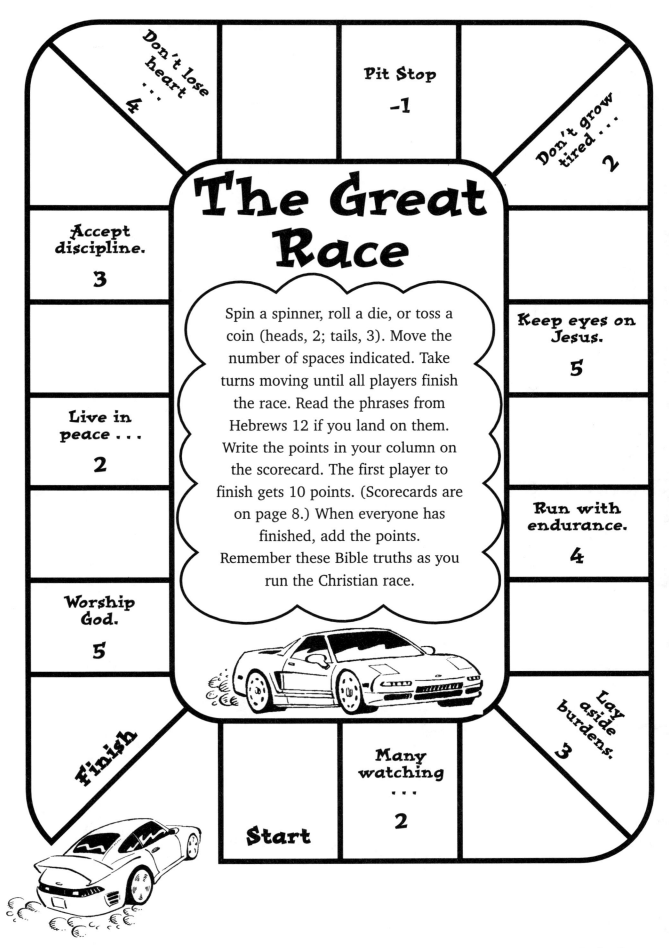

The Sower

Read this parable Jesus taught in Matthew 13:1-23. Begin at start. Spin a spinner, roll a die, or toss a coin (heads, 2; tails, 3). Move the number of spaces indicated. Take turns moving until a player reaches the garden. As you move, read the parable parts and give the explanations the game asks. Winner is first to reach A Winning Garden!

- Start
- Jesus tells a story. Matthew 13:1-9
- A farmer planted seeds.
- Some seed fell by the path.
- Some seed fell on rocky places.
- Birds ate some seed.
- Sun dried out some plants.
- Some seed fell in weeds.
- Weeds choked good plants.
- Some seed fell in good soil.
- Plants grew into grain.
- Explain seed by the path. Matthew 13:19
- Explain seed on rocky places. Matthew 13:20, 21
- Explain seed in weeds. Matthew 13:22
- Explain seed in good soil. Matthew 13:23
- A Winning Garden

2-4 players

© 1998 The Standard Publishing Company. Permission granted to photocopy for ministry use only—not for resale.

The Lost Son

Start

Dad loves family.

Son asks Dad for money.

Go ahead 1.

Dad gives money.

Go ahead 1.

Son moves away.

Go back 1.

Son throws parties...

spends all his money...

goes broke!

Go back 2.

Son eats pigs' food.

feeding pigs corn.

Son gets a job...

Now he's hungry!

Son decides to go home!

Go ahead 3.

Son is sorry.

Dad loves son.

Dad forgives.

Home!

Read stories about a lost coin, a lost sheep, and a lost son in Luke 15. This story Jesus taught is in Luke 15:11-32.

Spin a spinner, roll a die, or toss a coin (heads, 2; tails, 3). Move the number of spaces indicated. Take turns moving until a player gets home. Read the story parts when you land on them. The winner should explain the parable meaning.

© 1998 The Standard Publishing Company. Permission granted to photocopy for ministry use only—not for resale.

2-4 players

The Builder

Begin at start. Spin a spinner, roll a die, or toss a coin (heads, 2; tails, 3). Move the number of spaces indicated. Take turns moving until a player reaches the winning space. As you move, read the parable parts. The winner explains the meaning of the parable.

2-4 players

© 1998 The Standard Publishing Company. Permission granted to photocopy for ministry use only—not for resale.

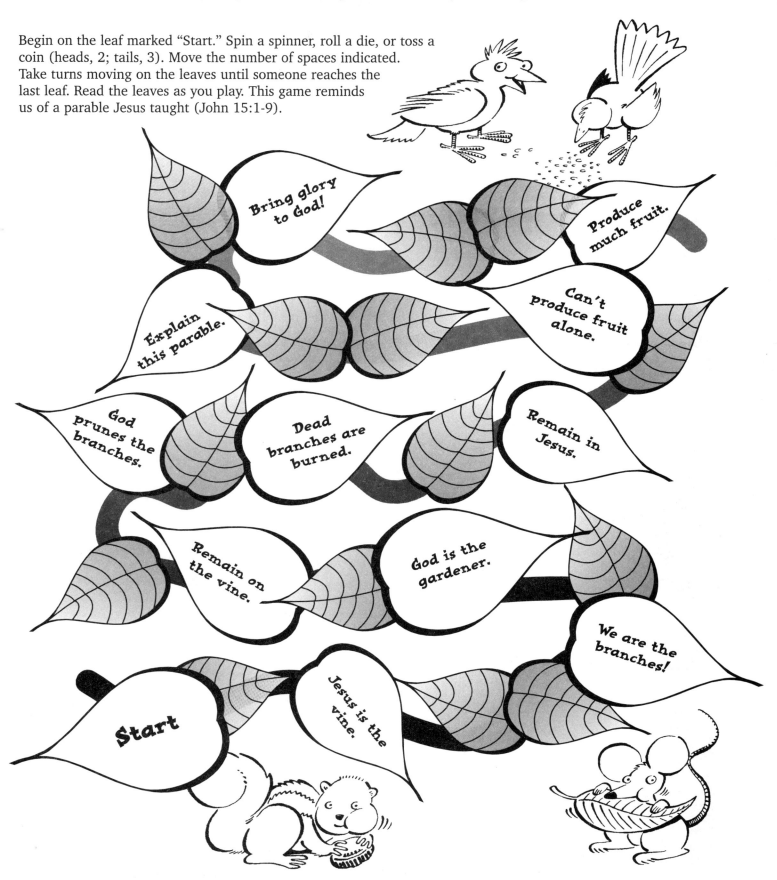

These four exciting games encourage learning and provide review with a minimum of teacher preparation.

Each game includes a blank set of question cards. The blank question cards can be used for additional verse questions (or questions based on other Bible translations). Photocopy the blank cards and type on your own questions. Then photocopy your question card pages, cut, and separate.

Fifteen to twenty-four questions provide enough challenge. Too few questions get repetitious and shorten the life of the game. The age level for each game can be adapted by the difficulty level of questions. Teachers can read simple questions to early readers.

Photocopy the master game board and question cards so that each group of two to four players has its own board and card set. Place question cards in an envelope to eliminate sorting card sets each time a game is played.

Both *Honeycomb* and the *One Another* game provide a Scripture page for players to read before they begin to play. Scripture is quoted from the *International Children's Bible*. Provide Bibles or the Scripture page for each player.

"B" Is for Bible game board
page 18

"B" Is for Bible

This game can be used to review general Bible information. Just select a topic, identify the ideas or facts to be reviewed, put those items in question form, type onto the photocopied blank question cards, photocopy, cut apart, and play.

To get you started, thirty-six question cards related to general Bible knowledge are provided (pages 19-21).

Each team will need a game board (page 18); a set of question cards (pages 19–22); a spinner, die, or coin; move tokens; a scorecard (page 8); and pencils.

One Another

One Another game board
page 25

This game teaches Scriptural principles of how Christians should behave toward one another. Players and teacher should read and discuss the "One Another Verses" before playing the game.

For each group, provide a game board (page 25); copies of "One Another Verses" (page 24); a spinner, die, or coin; move tokens; a set of question cards (pages 26-28); an optional scorecard (page 8); and pencils. If you want to use a scorecard, assign points for each question answered correctly.

This game differs from most games in that players may move in any direction to reach the Finish space.

Honeycomb

Honeycomb game board
page 31

This game reviews attitudes of Christian living from Jesus' Sermon on the Mount, Matthew 5:1-12.

Players and teacher should read and discuss "The Beatitudes" before beginning play. Each player should have a "Beatitude" worksheet or Bible to refer to during the game.

Blank bee question cards on page 34 allow teachers to use other questions or the wording from other Bible translations for questions. Photocopy the blank bee question cards, type questions on the cards, and then photocopy sets of new question cards.

For each group, provide a game board (page 31); copies of "The Beatitudes" verses (page 30) or a Bible; a spinner, die, or coin; move tokens; a set of bee question cards; a scorecard (page 8); and pencils.

Play Ball!

Play Ball! game board
page 36

Here's an all-purpose game board that elementary children enjoy.

This game board can be used to review nearly any Bible lesson or topic.

Photocopy the pitch ball questions (page 37). Type questions on the blank pitch ball cards. Plan to have at least sixteen questions. Photocopy the page of questions, enough for each group to have a set. Cut apart and place in envelopes.

When playing, place the pitch ball questions face down in the middle of the ball diamond on the game board.

For each group, provide a game board (page 36); a spinner, die, or coin; move tokens; pitch ball questions; and pencils.

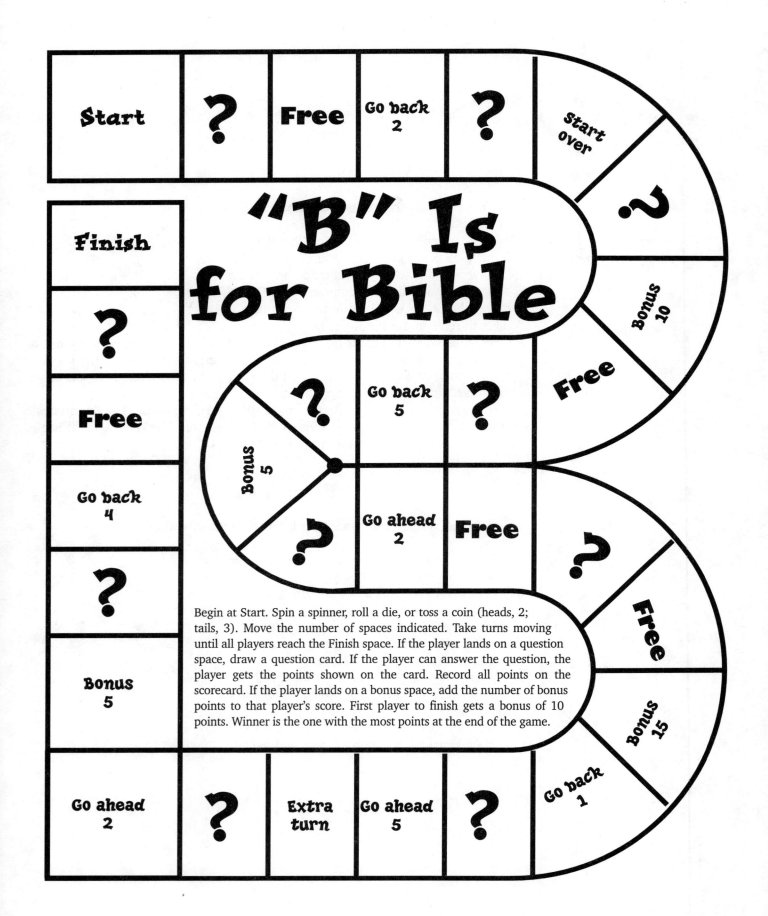

Bible Question Cards

1) Which Old Testament book tells about creation? 5 points	2) Which New Testament book tells of the second coming of Christ to the earth? 5 points	3) What man suffered greatly in a contest between God and Satan? 10 points
4) Which Old Testament book is a collection of wise sayings from a king? 5 points	5) Name two New Testament books that tell about Jesus' birth. 5 points	6) What Old Testament book is written as a poem of love? 10 points
7) Which Old Testament book tells about a prophet who disobeyed God and prayed while in a fish? 5 points	8) Which book tells about an Old Testament prophet who understood visions (and was thrown to lions)? 5 points	9) Name the longest and shortest Bible books. Which is from the Old Testament? Which is from the New Testament? 10 points
10) How many books are in the Bible? 5 points	11) Paul wrote to many Christians. Name three towns in which they lived. 5 points	12) Name the last book of the Old Testament. Is it a book of history or a book of prophecy? 10 points

© 1998 The Standard Publishing Company. Permission granted to photocopy for ministry use only—not for resale.

Bible Question Cards

---

13) Name the only New Testament book of prophecy.

5 points

---

14) Name two Old Testament prophets whose names are Bible books.

5 points

---

15) What are "epistles" and who wrote many of them?

10 points

---

16) What book of Old Testament history tells the story of a Jewish girl who saved her people?

5 points

---

17) Are the "gospels" in the Old or New Testament? Name them.

5 points

---

18) Who wrote the New Testament's book of prophecy, Revelation?

10 points

---

19) Name one book of poetry from the Old Testament.

5 points

---

20) Who wrote many of the Old Testament Psalms?

5 points

---

21) Name the New Testament history book that tells about the early church. Who wrote it?

10 points

---

22) Name the Old Testament book of prophecy that tells of Jesus' birth.

5 points

---

23) Who wrote most of the letters to early Christians telling how to live the Christian life?

5 points

---

24) Name the man who wrote the third Gospel book. What was his job or profession?

10 points

Bible Question Cards

25) Which Old Testament book gives the Ten Commandments? **5 points**	26) Which Old Testament book tells about a widow who loved and helped her mother-in-law and served her God? **5 points**	27) Name the five books of law. Which tells about building the tabernacle? **10 points**
28) Who wrote the first New Testament book? What was his profession before following Jesus? **5 points**	29) Name three of Paul's letters. **5 points**	30) Many of Paul's letters were written while he was a prisoner in the city of _____. **10 points**
31) Which Old Testament book prophesies Christ's death on the cross? **5 points**	32) Name the Bible book that tells of Peter taking the gospel to the Gentiles after a vision. **5 points**	33) Which Old Testament book tells how David defeated Goliath? **10 points**
34) Which New Testament book contains the "Sermon on the Mount"? **5 points**	35) Which four New Testament books tell about Jesus' miracles? **5 points**	36) Which New Testament book and chapter is called the "love" chapter? **10 points**

Question Card Forms

10 points	10 points	10 points	10 points
5 points	5 points	5 points	5 points
5 points	5 points	5 points	5 points

To make an answer key for each group leader, photocopy the answer key or photocopy a card set and add the answers.

'B' Is for BIBLE
answers for question card sets

1) Genesis
2) Revelation
3) Job
4) Proverbs
5) Matthew, Luke
6) Song of Solomon
7) Jonah
8) Daniel
9) Longest—Psalms, Old Testament; Shortest—2 John, New Testament
10) 66
11) *Choose:* Corinth, Ephesus, Thessalonica, Philippi, Rome
12) Malachi, prophecy
13) Revelation
14) *Choose:* Isaiah, Jeremiah, Ezekiel through Malachi
15) Letters, Paul
16) Esther
17) New Testament; Matthew, Mark, Luke, John
18) John
19) *Choose:* Job, Psalms, Proverbs, Ecclesiastes, Song of Solomon
20) David
21) Acts, Luke
22) Isaiah
23) Paul
24) Luke, physician
25) Exodus
26) Ruth
27) Genesis, Exodus, Leviticus, Numbers, Deuteronomy; Leviticus
28) Matthew; tax collector
29) *Choose:* Romans through Philemon
30) Rome
31) Isaiah
32) Acts
33) 1 Samuel
34) Matthew
35) Matthew, Mark, Luke, John
36) 1 Corinthians 13

© 1998 The Standard Publishing Company. Permission granted to photocopy for ministry use only—not for resale.

One Another Verses

"We are many, but in Christ we are all one body. Each one is a part of that body. And each part belongs to all the other parts."
Romans 12:5

"Love each other like brothers and sisters."
Romans 12:10

"Give your brothers and sisters more honor than you want for yourselves."
Romans 12:10

"Patience and encouragement come from God. And I pray that God will help you all agree with each other the way Christ Jesus wants."
Romans 15:5

"Christ accepted you, so you should accept each other. This will bring glory to God."
Romans 15:7

"I am sure that you are full of goodness. I know that you have all the knowledge you need and that you are able to teach each other."
Romans 15:14

"Greet each other with a holy kiss."
Romans 16:16

"God called you to be free. But do not use your freedom as an excuse to do the things that please your sinful self. Serve each other with love."
Galatians 5:13

"Help each other with your troubles. When you do this, you truly obey the law of Christ."
Galatians 6:2

"Always be humble and gentle. Be patient and accept each other with love."
Ephesians 4:2

"Be kind and loving to each other. Forgive each other just as God forgave you in Christ."
Ephesians 4:32

"Be willing to obey each other. Do this because you respect Christ."
Ephesians 5:21

"So comfort each other and give each other strength."
1 Thessalonians 5:11

Scriptures quoted from *International Children's Bible* (ICB)
© 1998 The Standard Publishing Company. Permission granted to photocopy for ministry use only—not for resale.

The One Another Game

"One Another" game cards

Left 6	Up 2	Finish
Right 1	Start Over	Left 3
Start	Down 3	Up 2

Read the "One Another" verses. Place game cards face down. Spin a spinner, roll a die, or toss a coin (heads, 2; tails, 3). Move the number of spaces indicated. Take turns moving until a player reaches the Finish space. Move in any direction but do what the space on which you land says. If you land on a ✾ space, draw a card and answer the question. First one at the Finish space wins.

2-4 players

One Another Question Cards

 Ephesians 4:32

1) Name ways Christians can show each other affection.

 Galatians 6:2

7) When we help each other, what have we obeyed?

 Galatians 5:13

2) What did God call us to be?

 Ephesians 4:2

8) We should always be _____ and _____ .

 Galatians 5:13

3) What should we not use our freedom in Christ to do?

 Ephesians 4:2

9) We should be _____ with each other and accept each other with _____ .

 Galatians 5:13

4) How can we best use the freedom God gave us?

 Ephesians 5:21

10) How can we show that we respect Christ?

 Galatians 5:13

5) In what way should we serve each other?

 1 Thessalonians 5:11

11) Name two things Christians should do for each other.

 Galatians 6:2

6) When another Christian has trouble, what should we do?

 Romans 12:10

12) Name a way Christians can treat each other as brothers and sisters in Christ.

One Another Question Cards

 Romans 12:10

13) In what way are we to love each other?

 Romans 15:5

19) Why is it important that Christians get along?

 Romans 12:10

14) Name a way we can give honor to our brothers and sisters in Christ.

 Romans 15:7

20) Who always loves and accepts us?

 Romans 12:5

15) How are we all part of one body?

 Romans 15:7

21) Why should we accept others as they are?

 Romans 12:5

16) Why should we take good care of our own body?

 Romans 15:7

22) What does God get when we accept each other?

 Romans 12:5

17) Give an example of caring for someone who is part of the body of Christ.

 Romans 15:14

23) Paul assures Christians that they are full of ____ .

 Romans 15:5

18) Who wants us to agree with each other?

 Romans 15:14

24) When Christians have knowledge, what can they do?

One Another Question Card Forms

To make an answer key for each group leader, photocopy the answer key or photocopy a card set and add the answers.

One Another
answers for question card sets

1) Kind, loving, forgiving
2) Free
3) Please our sinful selves
4) Serve each other with love
5) With love
6) Help each other
7) The law of Christ
8) Gentle, humble
9) Patient, love
10) Obey each other
11) Comfort, give strength
12) *Accept any correct response*
13) Like brothers and sisters
14) *Accept any correct response*
15) In Christ
16) We belong to others in Christ's body
17) *Accept any correct response*
18) Christ Jesus
19) *Accept any correct response*
20) Christ
21) Christ has accepted us
22) Glory
23) Goodness
24) Teach each other

© 1998 The Standard Publishing Company. Permission granted to photocopy for ministry use only—not for resale.

The Beatitudes

Matthew 5:1–12, ICB

1 Jesus saw the crowds who were there. He went up on a hill and sat down. His followers came to him.

2 Jesus taught the people and said:

3 "Those people who know they have great spiritual needs are happy. The kingdom of heaven belongs to them.

4 Those who are sad now are happy. God will comfort them.

5 Those who are humble are happy. The earth will belong to them.

6 Those who want to do right more than anything else are happy. God will fully satisfy them.

7 Those who give mercy to others are happy. Mercy will be given to them.

8 Those who are pure in their thinking are happy. They will be with God.

9 Those who work to bring peace are happy. God will call them his sons.

10 Those who are treated badly for doing good are happy. The kingdom of heaven belongs to them.

11 People will say bad things about you and hurt you. They will lie and say all kinds of evil things about you because you follow me. But when they do these things to you, you are happy.

12 Rejoice and be glad. You have a great reward waiting for you in heaven. People did the same evil things to the prophets who lived before you."

Use with the "Honeycomb" game.

© 1998 The Standard Publishing Company. Permission granted to photocopy for ministry use only—not for resale.

Honeycomb

Read Matthew 5:1-12 for the answers to this game. Place the bee question cards face down. Begin at Start. Spin a spinner, roll a die, or toss a coin (heads, 2; tails, 3). Move the number of spaces along the white path. Take turns moving until all players have finished. Draw a bee question card when you land on a bee. If you answer correctly, write your points on the scorecard. First player to finish gets 10 extra points. Winner is the one with the most points. Have a good "attitude"!

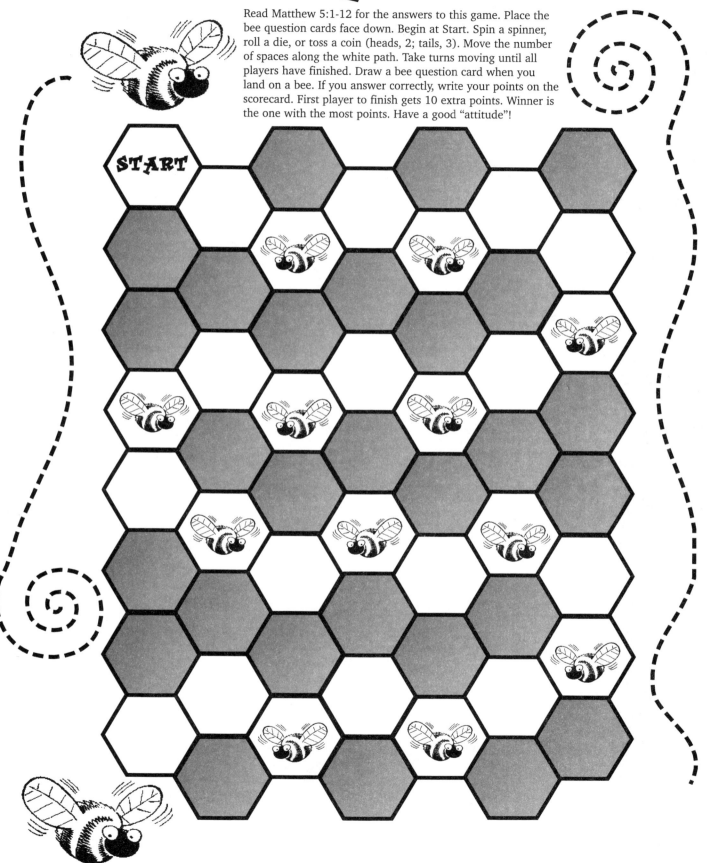

2-4 players

Bee Question Cards

1) Who taught the crowds from a hillside? **4 pts.**

2) Who was with Jesus while he taught the crowds of people? **3 pts.**

3) What is the name of the sermon from which the "Beatitudes" were taken? **5 pts.**

4) Why are people who know they have great spiritual needs happy? **2 pts.**

5) Why will those people who are sad be happy later? **4 pts.**

6) What does it mean to be humble? **3 pts.**

7) What will belong to all the humble people? **5 pts.**

8) What will God do for those who want to do right more than anything else? **2 pts.**

9) What will be given to those who give mercy to others? **4 pts.**

10) How should our thinking be? **3 pts.**

11) Where will people with pure thoughts be? **5 pts.**

12) What can Christians do to be called God's sons? **2 pts.**

© 1998 The Standard Publishing Company. Permission granted to photocopy for ministry use only—not for resale.

Bee Question Cards

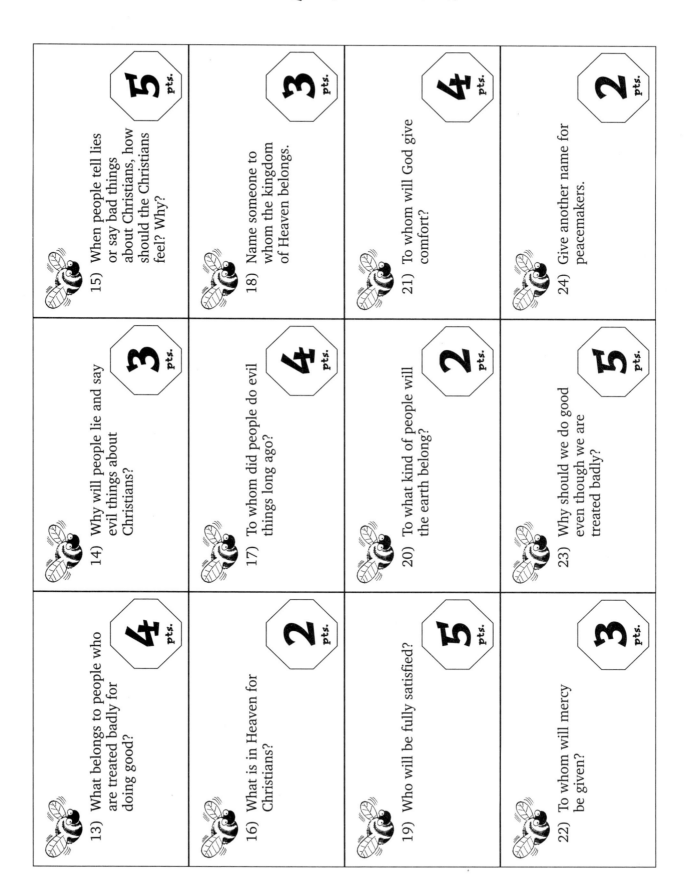

Bee Question Card Forms

34

Honeycomb
answers for question card sets

1) Jesus
2) His followers
3) The Sermon on the Mount
4) The kingdom of Heaven belongs to them
5) God will comfort them
6) *Accept any correct response*
7) The earth
8) Satisfy them
9) Mercy
10) Pure
11) With God
12) Work to bring peace
13) A great reward
14) Because they follow Jesus
15) Glad because of a great reward in Heaven
16) A great reward
17) The prophets
18) Those with spiritual needs
19) Those who want to do right
20) The humble
21) Those who are sad
22) Those who give mercy to others
23) For a great reward
24) God's children

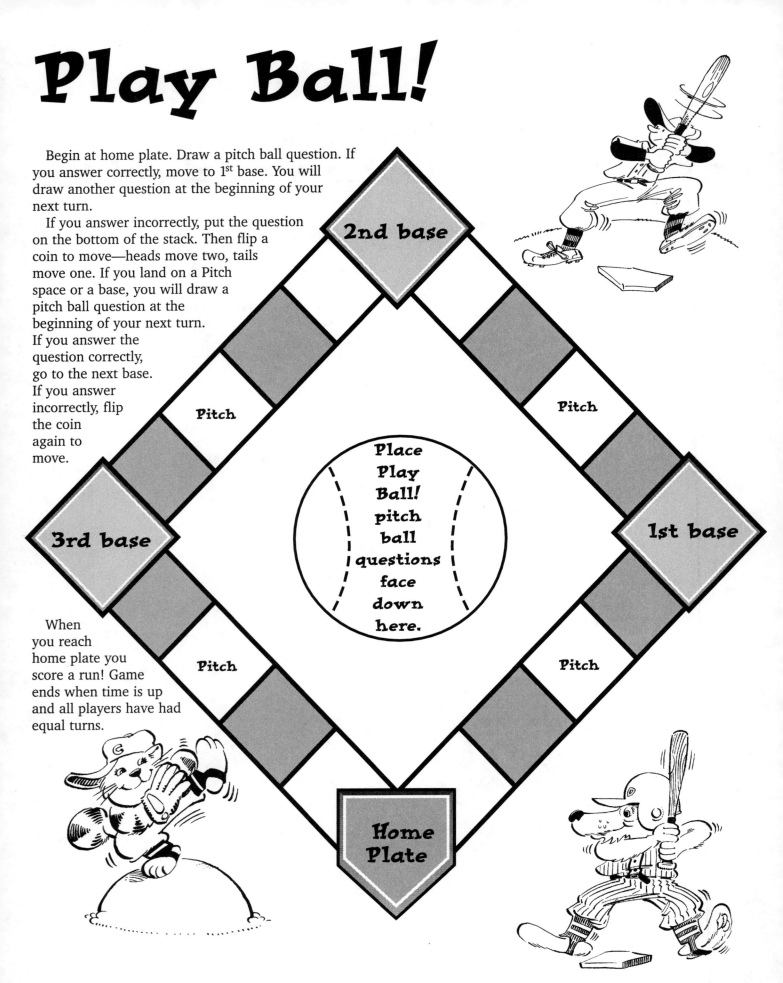

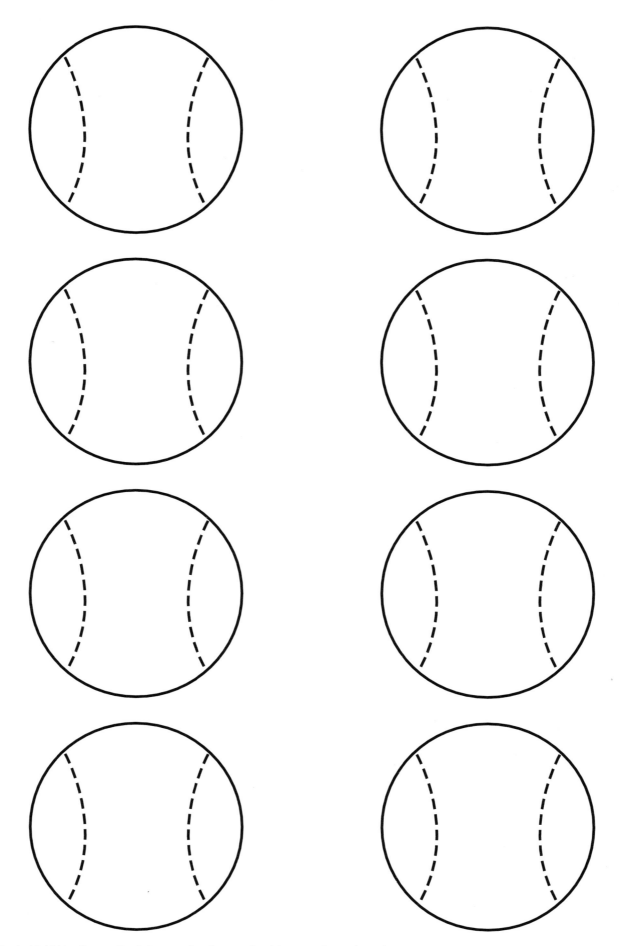

Bingo Bible Games

For any number of players

Bingo games provide a great way to teach and review!

Learn to recognize and pronounce names of books in the Old and New Testament, of men and women of the Bible, and of Bible places. Memorize the fruit of the Spirit or other Bible information.

Two Bingo forms are provided. Page 40 has sixteen squares and page 41 has twenty-five squares. Compile a list of items for the Bingo form you choose. If the list of items is less than the number of squares on the Bingo form, fill in the open squares with small stickers of Christian symbols such as the cross, Bible, or fish. Theme stickers may decorate those empty spaces—fruits for fruit of the Spirit and so on.

Fill in the squares randomly with the list you have chosen. Each form should be different. Older children can fill out their own forms by filling in their cards from a list you provide.

Copy each item from the list onto a small square of paper. Mix the squares and place them in a decorated container. The squares can be shaken, drawn, and called out. Also, prepare a master list so the leader can keep track of what has been called.

Small treats of gum, candy, or cookies make good prizes and keep interest high.

To make the Old or New Testament books game more interesting, copy the names on in different colors depending on their division: red for Gospels, blue for prophecy, green for letters, brown for law, etc.

Bible bingo lists may include many subjects. Here are some ideas.

Books of the Old or New Testament
Class members names
 (great for getting acquainted)
Names of current missionaries from
 your church
Names of hymns, choruses, or
 favorite songs
Animals of the Bible
Birds of the Bible
Cities of the Bible
Foods of the Bible
Jobs of the Bible

Miracles of the Bible
Places of the Bible
Plants of the Bible
Transportation in the Bible
Bible Names (of men, women,
 children)
Nations of Bible times
The twelve tribes of Israel
Ways to obey parents
Ways to show friendship
Ways to show kindness
Ways to help at church

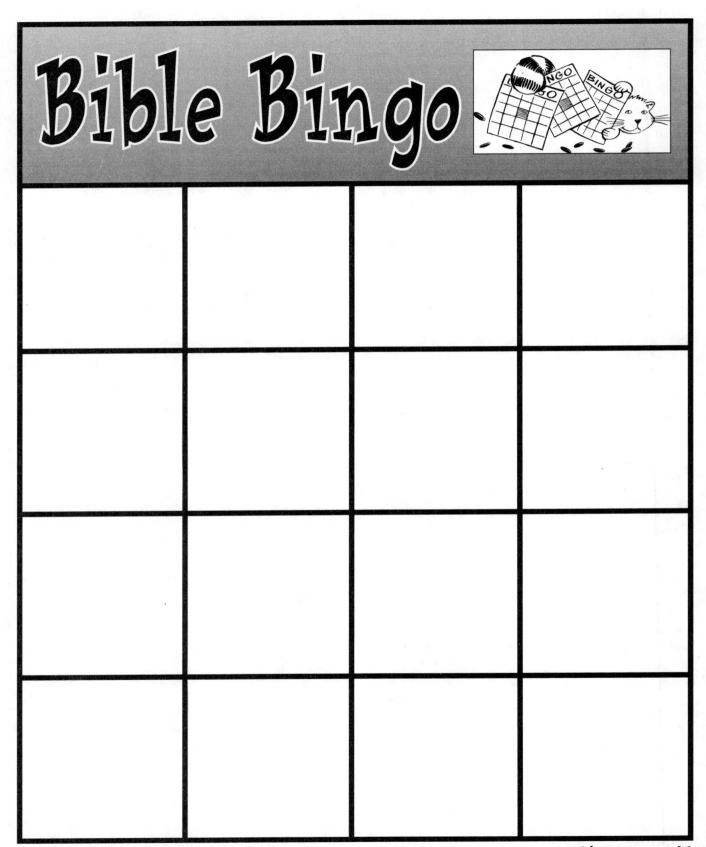

16-square grid

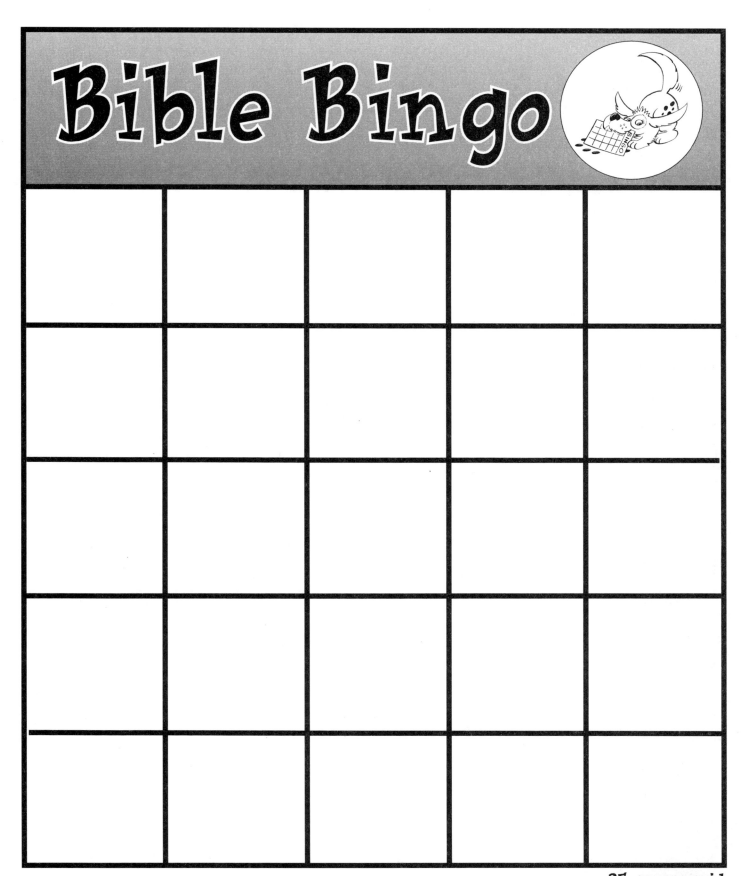

25-square grid

Overhead Projector Games

Overhead projector games provide another great way to add variety to your lessons and provide additional review time.

You will need a blank wall or screen, an overhead projector, transparencies made from game forms, washable transparency pens, and a list of questions or clues.

Initial Blocks

Photocopy the worksheet (page 46) and keep the master blank for future use.

Write clues appropriate for the age of the players. Use easy, well-known people or events for younger players. Use more complicated clues for teens and adults.

Complete directions for this game are on page 43.

Screen Scrabble

This unusual review game is similar to the board game "Scrabble." Forms (in two sizes) for photocopying are on pages 47 and 48.

Choose five or seven words from a lesson or topic list (depending on the age of players and amount of time for playing) and make up clues and an answer key.

Outline the first clue spaces on the transparency. Leave room for answers.

Divide the group in half to form two teams. Choose a captain and a secretary for each team. The secretary records letters named by a team. The captain announces the letter guesses and word guesses for a team.

Give Team 1 the first clue. Players on Team 1 choose letters until they miss a letter or guess the word correctly. If Team 1 misses, players on Team 2 choose until they miss a letter or guess the word correctly.

Alternate teams start each new word. On the last word, allow the losing team to start.

Each correct answer gets one point.

Build each new word from the preceding word. Outline the space and play.

SAMPLE GAME
Topic: Bible places
Clue 1   A nine-letter word that is the city with a special star.
Clue 2   Building on an E in Bethlehem, a five-letter word that names a place the Israelites left in a hurry.
Clue 3   Building on the T in Egypt, a seven-letter word naming a city Paul visited.
Clue 4   Building on the R in Corinth, a seven-letter word that names a city with shaky walls.
Clue 5   Building on the letter C in Jericho, a four-letter word that names the city where Jesus turned water into wine.

If you enjoy overhead Bible games, Standard Publishing offers two books of creative games: *Overhead Projector Games,* 14-03509; and *More! Overhead Projector Games,* 14-03510. Check with your local Christian bookstore.

Initial Blocks

You will need an initial block hexagon grid on an overhead transparency, overhead projector screen, or blank wall, and washable overhead transparency pens (black, red, blue).

1. Make a list of twenty Bible people, places, animals, things, books of the Bible, or combination of words related to recent lessons. The words will be used as answers.
   - Write twenty questions—one for each answer on your list.
   - Using a black pen, put the first initial from each of the twenty answers in the hexagons, one to each shape until all answers and hexagons are used.
   - If three or four names begin with the same letter, make certain that the question will make clear what the answer should be (e.g., Jesus, Joseph, Judas, James).
   - Place your transparency grid on an overhead projector.

2. Divide the group into two teams. Appoint a captain for the Red team and one for the Blue team.
   - Red team must go across the honeycomb in a zigzag line of touching hexagons. Red team must have a minimum of five hexagons touching across to win.
   - Blue team goes from top to bottom or vice versa. Blue team needs four or more hexagons touching to win.
   - Teams alternate turns. When they answer correctly, color the hexagon their color. If they miss, however, the opposing team gets a chance to answer that question.
   - If the opposition answers correctly, that team's color is placed in the hexagon. This makes a block. (This chance to place a block is not the opposition team's normal turn.)

3. Play the game.
   - Red team begins play. The Red team decides which letter (hexagon) to try.
   - The Red team's captain calls out the letter chosen by the team. The corresponding question is asked.
   - If it is answered correctly, color the shape red. If not, the Blue team tries to block by answering correctly.
   - Then Blue team plays its normal turn.
   - If no one guesses the correct answer, color it black. It becomes a block to both teams.
   - First team to cross the grid in their direction wins.

Initial Blocks

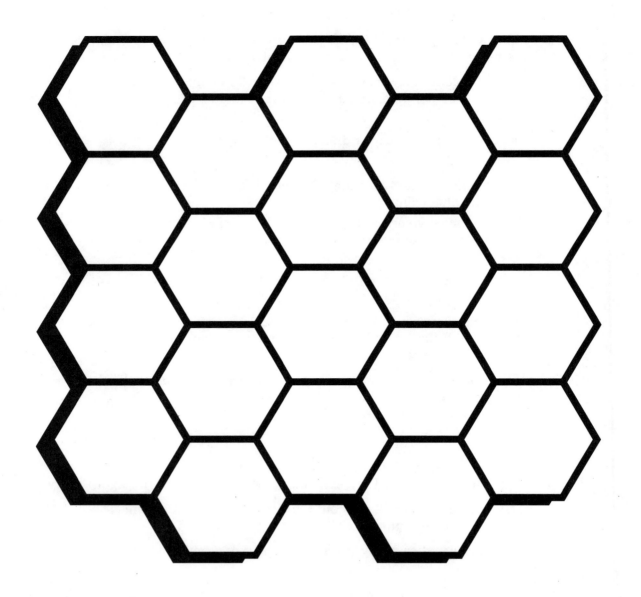

Initial Blocks

Here's a sample game to illustrate how to play. The clues may be given as questions or as the short phrase statements shown here.

Sample Topic: Men of the Bible

COLUMN ONE
  ADAM
  First man
  SAMUEL
  Called of God as a child
  JONAH
  Prophet swallowed by great fish
  METHUSELAH
  Old man

COLUMN TWO
  JESUS
  Son of God
  CAIN
  First murderer
  DANIEL
  Faced the lions
  JOHN THE BAPTIST
  Lost his head (or)
    Jesus' cousin

COLUMN THREE
  PAUL
  Writer of many New Testament books
  TIMOTHY
  Paul's young friend
  JUDAS
  Betrayed Jesus with a kiss
  ISAIAH
  Old Testament prophet who foretold
    Christ's death

COLUMN FOUR
  BARNABAS
  Traveled with Paul on missionary journeys
  PETER
  Cut off a soldier's ear
  SOLOMON
  A wise king
  MATTHEW
  A converted tax collector

COLUMN FIVE
  DAVID
  Killed a giant with a stone
  MOSES
  Hidden in the tall grass by the Nile
  BARABBAS
  Released instead of Jesus
  LUKE
  New Testament doctor

Sample overhead sheet for this game

© 1998 The Standard Publishing Company. Permission granted to photocopy for ministry use only—not for resale.

Initial Blocks Worksheet

Topic _____

Column One

Answer _____

Clue _____

_____

Answer _____

Clue _____

_____

Answer _____

Clue _____

_____

Answer _____

Clue _____

_____

Column Three

Answer _____

Clue _____

_____

Answer _____

Clue _____

_____

Answer _____

Clue _____

_____

Answer _____

Clue _____

_____

Column Five

Answer _____

Clue _____

_____

Answer _____

Clue _____

_____

Answer _____

Clue _____

_____

Answer _____

Clue _____

_____

Column Two

Answer _____

Clue _____

_____

Answer _____

Clue _____

_____

Answer _____

Clue _____

_____

Answer _____

Clue _____

_____

Column Four

Answer _____

Clue _____

_____

Answer _____

Clue _____

_____

Answer _____

Clue _____

_____

Answer _____

Clue _____

_____

© 1998 The Standard Publishing Company. Permission granted to photocopy for ministry use only—not for resale.

SCREEN SCRABBLE

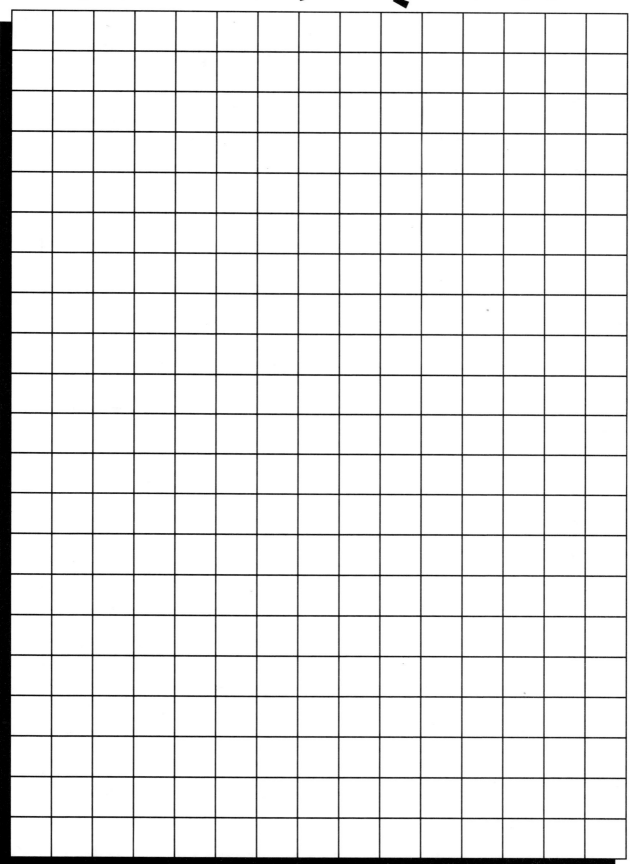

315 squares

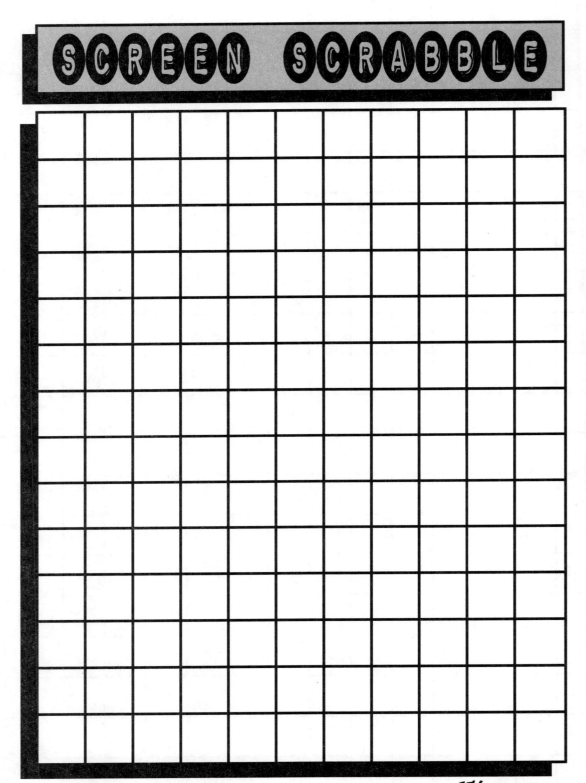